The Music Scene

The History of Modern Music

Matt Anniss

A+
Smart Apple Media

Published by Smart Apple Media, an imprint of
Black Rabbit Books
P.O. Box 3263, Mankato, Minnesota 56002
www.smartapplemedia.com

Published by arrangement with the Watts Publishing
Group LTD, London.

Library of Congress Cataloging-in-Publication Data
Anniss, Matt.
 The history of modern music / Matt Anniss.
    pages cm. – (The music scene)
 Includes index.
 Summary: "Describes the history of popular music
genres, starting with the rock-and-roll movement of
the 1950s. Explains how genres have been created
based on social and cultural events through recent
history. Case studies highlight how world events and
technology influenced artists that led new genres of
music"–Provided by publisher.
 ISBN 978-1-59920-910-4 (library binding)
 1. Popular music–History and criticism–Juvenile
literature. I. Title.
 ML3470.A56 2015
 781.6409'045–dc23
                        2012043918

ISBN 978-1-59920-910-4 (library binding)
ISBN 978-1-62588-590-6 (eBook)

Dewey classification: 781.6'4'09

Printed in the United States by CG Book Printers
North Mankato, Minnesota

PO 1720
PO 2-2015

9 8 7 6 5 4 3 2 1

Acknowledgments:
The publisher would like to thank the following
for permission to reproduce photographs: Corbis:
Sunset Boulevard 19t; Dreamstime: Mira Agron
38, Rui Dias Aidos 18, Larisa Chernisheva 35br,
Howsat 17, Imagecollect 41, Joyfull 35t, Pressureua
42, Stormarn 15t; Getty Images: Redferns 13;
iStockphoto: EdStock2 29bl, D Withers 14; Library
of Congress: Herman Hiller 12t, Warren K Leffler
12bl, Metro-Goldwyn-Mayer Inc 6, United Press
International 10; Rex Features: 28, Kevin Cole 8,
Everett Collection 36, Terry O'Neill 9, Sheila Rock
22t, Richard Young 22b, 27; Shutterstock: Admedia
32t, Anthony Correia 39b, Excellent backgrounds
33, Andrija Kovac 19b, Aija Lehtonen 23, Northfoto
25tl, 34, 43b, Oliveromg 5, 40, Ferenc Szelepcsenyi
21b, Jeff Thrower cover; Spotify: 43tr; Wikipedia:
2xUeL 26, A l'origine 31, Joel Brodksy/Electra
Records 15br, Bryan Coastales 16, Will Fresch 37b,
Simon Green 30-31, Joho34 25r, Klau Klettner/Hydra
Records 7, Lola's Big Adventure! 37r, Wolfgang
Moroder 24, Masao Nakagami 32bl, Notorious TF
21tr, Scootie 30b, Squelle 29tr, Deborah Wilbanks 39l.

Every attempt has been made to clear copyright.
Should there be any inadvertent omission please
apply to the publisher for rectification.

CONTENTS

CHAPTER ONE

THE BIRTH OF MODERN MUSIC

At the end of World War II in 1945, few would have believed that within 10 years a musical revolution would take place in the United States. In the mid-1950s, a new form of music took the world by storm and set in motion an uprising of musical adventure and experimentation. This new music was rock and roll.

Divided Nation

In the years following World War II, the United States was still a nation divided by strict **race laws**. Black people did not have the same freedoms as white people, and were considered by the **racist system** as second-class citizens. Because of this, the musical sounds and traditions of the country's black and white populations were kept separate.

Joining Together

In the early 1950s, white musicians began to make music that was heavily influenced by traditionally black styles, such as **rhythm and blues** and **jazz**. The first genre to **fuse** black and white music styles was rockabilly. This was a combination of the heavy beats and rhythms of blues, folk, and country music influences.

Enter Elvis

In 1954, Elvis Presley, a former trucker from Memphis, Tennessee, had a worldwide hit with a rockabilly song called "That's Alright Mama." Teenagers loved the song, and Elvis quickly became the headline star of a worldwide rock and roll revolution.

Rock Around the Clock

Rock and roll was slightly different from rockabilly. It featured electric instruments and was similar to rhythm and blues. It was first made popular by Bill Haley and the Comets, whose 1955 song "Rock Around the Clock" became a worldwide hit.

The scoop

Although "Rock Around the Clock" and "That's Alright Mama" were huge hits, many music historians think that Little Richard's "Tutti Frutti" was the song that really kick-started rock and roll. Recorded and released in 1955, its simple energy and heavy sound inspired a whole new generation of would-be stars.

Bill Haley's fun songs helped to make rock and roll a worldwide phenomenon in the 1950s.

Teenage Kicks

There were two things about rock and roll that made it attractive to teenagers. First, it was music they could dance to. Second, their parents hated it! The older generation couldn't understand the music's raw power and loud **chords**, and just made teenagers love rock and roll even more. It was something that was "theirs" and separated them from their parents.

Revolution in Sound

For the first time ever, buying, playing, and listening to music became an essential part of being a teenager. Rock and roll changed the way teenagers dressed, spoke, and how they spent their spare time. Sales of vinyl records soared and organized rock and roll dances, often called "sock hops," became the place to be seen. In the future, nothing would be the same again. Today's bands might not make rock and roll, but without these 1950s pioneers, we would have no rock music at all.

THE BRITISH ARE COMING

American rock and roll ruled in the late 1950s, but by the mid-1960s the world was dancing to different sounds. They came from the United Kingdom, specifically the cities of Liverpool and Manchester.

The biggest rock and pop stars of the 1960s were followed by fanatical groups of screaming teenage fans.

A New Sound

Rock and roll had a big effect on many British teenagers. But it was a British version of rock and roll called "skiffle" that made the biggest impact. Skiffle was played with **acoustic** instruments rather than electric ones, and it was made popular by the singer Lonnie Donegan. Inspired by both skiffle and Elvis, many teenagers formed their own bands.

A New Beat

By the early 1960s, many skiffle bands had "gone electric" and replaced their homemade music-making equipment with instruments. These young bands began to make a form of pop music that was influenced by rock and roll, but kept a very British sound. It was called "beat music." Nowhere was beat music more popular than in Liverpool.

From The Cavern to the Charts

The beat music scene in Liverpool was based around a music venue called The Cavern Club. It was here that many local bands first played and where they perfected their sound.

The Scoop

One of the most successful Merseybeat bands of the early 1960s was Gerry and the Pacemakers. They set a record when their first three singles reached number one on the British charts. No one had ever done that before—not even The Beatles!

8

One of these bands, The Beatles, rose up the British charts in 1964. Record labels quickly rushed to sign more groups from Liverpool, and soon these groups, nicknamed "Merseybeat bands" ruled the charts.

The Invasion Begins

It wasn't long before American teenagers began to get a taste for British beat music. In 1964, The Beatles made their first trip to the United States. After appearing on a popular television talk show, they were headline news. Their concerts sold out, and their music sold in record-breaking time. In one week in April 1964, The Beatles held the top five positions on the Billboard Top 100 chart.

British Blues

British pop music at the time was also greatly influenced by the heavier sound of American rhythm and blues. In London, a homegrown blues scene developed. Bands such as The Rolling Stones, The Kinks, and The Who gave audiences a sound that was far rougher than the clean-cut pop created by the Merseybeat bands. It wasn't long before these bands made their mark in the United States and led the way to a decade of dominance by British rock that lasted into the early 1970s. Even recent bands such as Oasis, Coldplay, and The Killers owe a debt to British pop of the 1960s.

Rule Britannia

Following The Beatles, many other British bands were successful in the United States. The American media called this "The British Invasion." Other than The Beatles, the US also fell in love with The Dave Clark Five, Freddie and the Dreamers, and Herman's Hermits.

The Rolling Stones are still making records today, over 50 years after recording their first song.

The Beatles

The Beatles are the most successful band ever. During the 1960s, John Lennon, Paul McCartney, Ringo Starr, and George Harrison recorded some of the best-known music of the time. They were the first pop band to achieve worldwide fame.

Between 1964 and 1970, The Beatles had an amazing 21 number-one hit singles in the United States and many more worldwide.

On the Rise

John Lennon and Paul McCartney formed The Beatles in the late 1950s. By 1962, they were big news in their home city of Liverpool, UK. Local businessman Brian Epstein discovered them and persuaded EMI Records to sign them.

Beatlemania

Thanks to a clean cut image and catchy pop songs in their own unique Merseybeat style, The Beatles became international stars in 1964. "Beatlemania" spread, and the band couldn't go anywhere without being followed by crowds of screaming fans.

Bright Stars

During 1964 and 1965, The Beatles were probably the most famous people on the planet. They starred in two successful films, *A Hard Day's Night* and *Help!*, and spent most of their time touring the world. They put on concerts in huge sports stadiums, playing their hit singles to crowds of teenage girls.

Studio Time

The Beatles soon tired of their fame and decided to stop touring in 1966. Instead, they focused on making music in the recording studio. They had already started making **experimental** music with the 1965 album *Rubber Soul*, but the albums that followed in 1966 and 1967 revolutionized the music industry.

New Sounds

With the aid of producer George Martin and almost unlimited studio time, The Beatles were able to venture into new sounds and recording techniques.

Making It Big

After The Beatles recorded their second single in London's Abbey Road studios, George Martin famously said, "Congratulations gentlemen, you've just made your first number-one record." He was proved right as "Please Please Me" rocketed to the top of the British charts.

Their 1966 album *Revolver* featured songs recorded with violins, cellos, traditional Indian instruments, and a soul-style **horn** section. Most **revolutionary** was a song called "Tomorrow Never Knows," which used cutting-edge tape **editing** and **looping techniques** that had rarely been heard before.

Everything Changes

Revolver and its follow-up *Sgt. Pepper's Lonely Hearts Club Band* had a huge impact. They showed not only the limitless potential of rock and pop music, but also what could be achieved in the recording studio. In the following years, albums became works of art—not just collections of songs.

TIMELINE: The Beatles

1957: Paul McCartney joins John Lennon's skiffle group, The Quarrymen
1960: The Quarrymen change their name to The Beatles
1962: "Love Me Do" single hits UK Top 20
1963: "Please Please Me" tops British charts

1964: Beatlemania sweeps the US
1966: *Revolver* album is released
1967: *Sgt. Pepper's Lonely Hearts Club Band* album is released
1970: The Beatles' final album, *Let It Be*, is released

SOUL POWER

In the 1950s, white Americans reinvented black forms of music. In the 1960s, black performers hit the pop charts with a style that crossed over into the mainstream—soul.

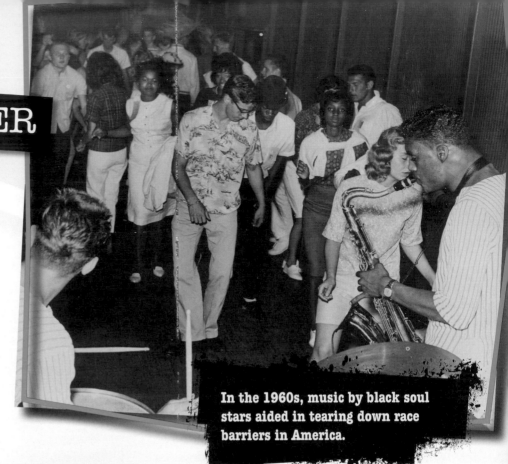

In the 1960s, music by black soul stars aided in tearing down race barriers in America.

The rise of soul music in the 1960s helped to spur on black Americans in their struggle for equal rights.

Difficult Times

The United States in the 1960s was a country still full of racial problems, with laws that did not allow basic human rights to black people. Even in these hard times, some black performers were able to become successful pop stars. Their success paved the way for future black performers to dominate the global music scene for years to come.

Got to Have Soul

Soul music first developed in the late 1950s in the northern US cities of Chicago and Detroit. There, singers and musicians had been raised on **gospel songs** in church. They used the heart they'd grown up with to develop a soulful version of rhythm and blues, which was popular in black communities at the time. The first soul singer to hit the big time was Ray Charles, who had many hit singles in the late 1950s.

Motown Begins

In 1959, a Detroit songwriter-turned-businessman named Berry Gordy decided to open two record labels called Tamla and Motown in a house that Gordy called Hitsville USA. Today, Hitsville USA is a museum.

Diana Ross and the Supremes were the first all-black girl group to conquer the American charts.

Motown Sounds

Many people believe that Berry Gordy, owner of the Tamla and Motown record labels, did the most to make soul music popular. Gordy got together with a group of great local songwriters and musicians and set out to make pop hits. He signed up **record producer** Norman Whitfield and a talented songwriting team called Holland-Dozier-Holland. Between them, they were able to create the Motown **trademark sound** that both white and black teenagers loved. Many Motown Records artists made it to the top of the Billboard Top 100 pop charts as a result.

Motown Stars

In the early 1960s, Motown Records had hits from artists such as Diana Ross and the Supremes, Martha and the Vandellas, Smokey Robinson and the Miracles, The Temptations, Marvin Gaye, and Tammy Tyrell. These artists became worldwide stars, as the Motown sound became popular in Europe and Australia, as well.

The Scoop

The first Motown Records single to hit number one in the US was The Marvelettes' "Please Mister Postman." It reached the top of the charts in 1961 and was later covered by The Beatles.

Motown Forever

The '60s soul sound of the Motown and Tamla labels continues to be popular to this day, and many current R&B and pop stars have been influenced by this period. Cee Lo Green, Amy Winehouse, and Mayer Hawthorne have all forged careers on the backs of records that borrow from the Motown feel. Even some big R&B records, such as Beyoncé's *Crazy in Love*, contain elements of long-forgotten 1960s soul records.

CHANGING TIMES

The late 1960s was a difficult time. World events such as the **Vietnam War** and the **assassination** of would-be president Robert Kennedy, plus social changes such as the hippie movement and the black civil rights movement, had a big effect on the music of the era.

Speaking Out

In the mid to late 1960s, an alternative (or **underground**) music movement was growing in the United States. **Folk** rock musicians such as Bob Dylan, Leonard Cohen, and Simon and Garfunkel expressed their thoughts on social and political issues through their music.

War Cry

Many musicians were inspired to create music that spoke about the Vietnam War. The conflict had been ongoing since the early 1960s, but it became big news when American soldiers were sent to the country in 1965. Many musicians felt strongly that the Vietnam War was wrong, and that the United States should not be involved.

Flower Power

A number of protest singers became part of an underground music and lifestyle scene in San Francisco, California, that became known as the "hippie movement." Hippies believed in peace, love, and individual freedom. Their message spread around the world. Many underground musicians—and even famous ones, such as The Beatles—shared their beliefs and included hippie ideals in the music they made.

Psychedelia

In the late 1960s, many musicians experimented with taking dangerous, **mind-altering** drugs, such as **LSD**. These drugs ruined many lives by seriously damaging people's mental and physical health. They also inspired some bands to make strange and exciting new rock, soul, and pop music. As a result, **psychedelic** rock was one of the biggest musical forms of the period.

The Beatles changed pop music forever with their psychedelic album *Sgt. Pepper's Lonely Hearts Club Band.*

The Scoop

Illegal drugs have destroyed the lives of a number of underground rock stars over the years. In 1970, guitarist Jimi Hendrix died at the age of 27 as a result of drugs. He was one of the brightest stars of underground music.

Into the 21st Century

In 2011, a new wave of folk rock bands began to climb up the charts. Acts such as Bon Iver, Mumford and Sons, and The Decemberists owe much to the 1970s sound of Bob Dylan and Simon and Garfunkel. Meanwhile, some strains of electronic music called ambient and trance, borrow elements from psychedelic music. Even heavy rockers such as The Red Hot Chili Peppers can trace their roots back to 1960s **funk**-rock!

Alternative Sounds

On both sides of the Atlantic, teenagers and young people were beginning to buy more music influenced by underground culture. In universities and colleges, students gathered to listen to bands such as The Doors and The Grateful Dead, who were known as **alternative rockers**. Meanwhile, already successful rock and pop acts such as The Beatles, The Who, and The Beach Boys, began to make records inspired by the psychedelic music that was taking over.

The Doors were one of the most successful early alternative rock bands, playing to packed audiences around the world.

Underground Goes Overground

By the end of the 1960s, alternative or "progressive" rock music had become one of the best-selling styles in the world. What was once thought of as underground music had become **mainstream**. It set a trend. In the future, many underground styles of music would cross over into the pop charts.

CHAPTER TWO

EVERYTHING CHANGES

Crowds flocked to see Jefferson Airplane at the Fantasy Fair and Magic Mountain Festival.

Music festivals occur each summer, with acts as big as Beyoncé, Jay-Z, U2, Coldplay, and Radiohead playing headline sets at huge events all around the world. It hasn't always been this way—until 1967, there were no rock and pop festivals at all.

Fantasy Festival

All modern music festivals can trace their beginnings back to an event in San Francisco, California, called the Fantasy Fair and Magic Mountain Festival. Headlined by Canned Heat, Captain Beefheart, and The Byrds, the festival took place over two days in June 1967. It marked the beginning of what has become known as rock music's "Summer of Love."

The Word Spreads

The following year, more music festivals began to spring up around the world. In the United States, two weekend-long events called the Miami Pop Festival were held at a race track in Florida. Meanwhile, 10,000 people traveled to a small island off the south coast of the United Kingdom for the first ever Isle of Wight Festival, which has since become one of the world's most popular festivals.

Trailblazers

While these festivals paved the way for the future, there were a number of events in 1969 that really put the rock festival concept on the map. Perhaps the most famous of all these festivals was Woodstock, a nonstop, three-day event that was held in rural New York.

Legendary Woodstock

Woodstock has become legendary for a number of reasons, one being the standout performances from Jefferson Airplane, Joan Baez, Sly and the Family Stone, and The Who, among others. It is estimated that over 500,000 people attended the Woodstock festival, giving it, even to date, one of the largest festival attendances ever.

The Scoop

One of the most talked-about performances in the history of rock music took place at the Woodstock festival in 1969. It came from guitarist Jimi Hendrix, who wowed festival-goers with a solo version of "The Star Spangled Banner." It has become one of rock music's most **iconic** moments.

Watching Dylan

In the United Kingdom, two festivals in 1969 also made a huge impact. One was the second Isle of Wight Festival, which attracted a record 150,000 people to see Bob Dylan play. It was the singer-songwriter's first live appearance since he had been injured in a motorcycle accident in 1968. Dylan's appearance was so anticipated that even members of The Beatles and The Rolling Stones turned up to watch the legendary performer.

Bath Blues

There was another festival that summer that was hugely important. Held in Bath, UK, the Bath Festival of Blues featured appearances from rhythm and blues bands such as Fleetwood Mac and John Mayall and the Bluesbreakers. More importantly, it inspired a farmer named Michael Eavis to host his own music festival—Glastonbury. Today, Glastonbury is a huge music event that captures a worldwide audience.

Glastonbury Begins

Michael Eavis hosted the first Glastonbury Festival on his farm in Pilton, UK, in September 1970. Tickets cost $1.60 (£1) and 1,500 people attended. The first band to play at the festival was a local group called Stackridge.

The Arcadia stage was one of more than 120 stages at the Glastonbury Festival of 2014.

RISE OF DISCO

During the 1970s, a new form of music took nightclubs by storm—disco. Its rise led to a boom in nightclubs, as well as the birth of the club DJ. In the process, dance music culture was born.

Disco Funk

Disco started to become a style of music in the mid-1970s. Musicians began to make longer soul and funk tracks to appeal to nightclub dancers. It wasn't long before a strong disco sound developed, featuring heavy drum beats, strings, funky **bass lines**, and soulful vocals.

The effects of disco music on fashion in the 1970s can still be seen today.

Rise of the DJ

In the clubs of New York City, groundbreaking DJs such as Francis Grasso, Nicky Siano, and Walter Gibbons realized they could create a seamless performance by matching the drum beats in two different records and mixing them together. Almost overnight, the DJ as we know it was created.

The Scoop

One of the world's longest-running disco events is called The Loft. These gigs were first held in the New York attic apartment of a music fan named David Mancuso in 1970. They are still going to this day, with similar events held in London and Tokyo.

Disco Spreads

In the mid- to late 1970s, disco spread beyond the underground nightclubs of New York City and Philadelphia. Popular clubs such as Studio 54 in New York, and hit records from artists such as Donna Summer, The Jacksons, and The Bee Gees, made disco a big hit worldwide. The number of people regularly going to nightclubs soared.

Night Fever

Disco hit the big screen in 1977 with the popular film *Saturday Night Fever*. This story about a New York teenager who escapes his troubles by becoming a champion disco dancer caught the imagination of audiences

18

around the world. The soundtrack album, featuring songs by The Bee Gees and The Trammps, is one of the best-selling albums of all time.

Big Comeback

The popularity of disco faded at the end of the 1970s, but by then, both DJing and nightclub culture had become widespread. In recent years, 1970s disco has become popular once more, as DJs and musicians such as Madonna, Rihanna, and Lady Gaga have rediscovered dance music.

Remix Culture

Today, many pop songs have extra-long versions designed to appeal to dancers in nightclubs. These are known as "remixes" and were first created in the disco era by a man named Tom Moulton. He made remixes especially for DJs, pressing them onto vinyl records in very small quantities. They were so popular that, in 1976, record labels began to release these records.

John Travolta's dancing in *Saturday Night Fever* turned the world on to disco music.

Disco DJs helped to turn playing records in clubs into an art form.

The Birth of Hip-Hop

New York in the 1970s was alive with new musical developments. Alongside disco, the city also created one of the biggest music styles of the twentieth century—hip-hop. This **pioneering** genre paved the way for current rap superstars such as Eminem, 50 Cent, and Lil Wayne.

Kool Beginnings

On August 11, 1973, a party took place at a community center in the Bronx neighborhood of New York City. The DJ for the night was a Jamaican-born music fan called Kool Herc. He amazed dancers by using two copies of the same record on two turntables to extend the song's heavy drum patterns. As he did this, he talked, or rapped, over the records on a microphone.

Bronx Block Parties

Soon, many other local DJs were copying Kool Herc's extended drum breaks at illegal outdoor **block parties** all over the Bronx. One DJ, Grandmaster Flash, went even further by refining "**quick mix**" **mixing** and inventing scratching—quickly moving a record backward and forward by hand to create a variety of noises.

TIMELINE: The birth of hip-hop

1973: DJ Kool Herc uses two records to extend sections of dance records

1976: DJ Grandmaster Flash unveils his "quick mix theory"

1977: Grandmaster Flash forms The Furious Five, the first established rap group

1978: Lovebug Starski becomes the first in-house rapper at the Disco Fever club in the Bronx

1979: The Sugarhill Gang records and releases "Rapper's Delight"

1979: Grandmaster Flash and the Furious Five release their "Superrappin'" single

20

Break Dance Beats

In the late 1970s, the roles of the DJ and the microphone man separated. DJs concentrated on creating a good atmosphere for local dance fans known as "break dancers," while MCs, or rappers, spoke in rhyme over the music.

Along with DJ Kool Herc, Grandmaster Flash invented turntable techniques that are still used by today's hip-hop DJs.

Good Times

In the early days of hip-hop, there was no single style of music used by DJs and rappers. DJs played a variety of music, focusing on the heavy drum breaks found in rock, disco, soul, funk, **Latin**, and pop.

Modern rappers such as Xzibit owe their livelihoods to New York's 1970s hip-hop pioneers.

History Maker

What hip-hop needed to go global was a hit record. That came in 1979. Businesswoman Sylvia Robinson heard hip-hop DJs and rappers at a party in New York and decided the time was right to record a rap record. She asked her recording studio's house band to record a **backing track** based on the groove from Chic's "Good Times." She then asked three New Jersey teenagers to add their own raps.

Rap Attack

Credited to The Sugarhill Gang, "Rapper's Delight" was released on November 9, 1979. The 15-minute rap record quickly became a huge smash worldwide, reaching the Top 10 in the United Kingdom, Germany, Canada, France, and Australia. In the months and years to come, more hip-hop records were released, and by the late 1980s rap music had become a global force.

ANGRY SOUNDS

During the 1970s, many teenagers in the United States turned their back on mainstream rock and pop music. Angry at the world around them, they created their own music—punk.

The Ramones blazed a trail by helping to invent an angry new form of rock music called punk.

Trouble Brewing

At this time, mainstream music was a mix of glam rock, over-the-top progressive rock, slick soul, and goodtime disco. Many teenagers felt this didn't fit in with their day-to-day lives. All they saw were fewer jobs for school dropouts and mass strikes by workers demanding better pay. They were angry about what was happening around them and needed a release.

Cult Heroes

Like many teenagers before them, young people turned to music. They began to make loud, simple, angry rock music. Two bands in New York led the way—The New York Dolls and The Ramones. These groups built up a cult following on both sides of the Atlantic and headed a new style called punk rock.

Punk Fever Spreads

It wasn't long before punk's influence spread to the United Kingdom. Punk scenes grew up in cities such as London, Manchester, Birmingham, and Sheffield. Led by bands such as The Clash, The Damned, and The Sex Pistols, punk's popularity quickly grew during 1976.

The Sex Pistols' angry antics made headlines all around the world, and set sales of punk records soaring.

22

The Scoop

In December 1976, The Sex Pistols sparked outrage in British newspapers following a live television interview. During the interview, guitarist Steve Jones repeatedly swore at host Bill Grundy. The shocking incident brought punk rock to wider public attention for the first time.

Anarchy in the UK

The UK's troubled summer of 1977 was filled with strikes and protests. At the same time, the punk rock movement represented the gap between teenagers, their parents, and "the establishment"—namely the police and politicians. The attitude of punk rockers and their simple-but-effective music inspired many British teenagers to form their own bands.

The Birth of "Indie"

Punk died out in the early 1980s, but its independent attitude lived on through independent rock and pop bands and record labels. They created the "indie" scene of today. Punk itself has been reinvented in recent years by "nu punk" and "skate punk" bands such as Green Day and Blink-182.

Punk's Legacy

Punk music is important because it gave a new boost to the idea of the independent record label. Many 1970s punk artists rejected big deals with major record labels, and instead made and released music themselves. This is something many bands still do today, distributing their music using popular websites and online services such as iTunes, SoundCloud, and Bandcamp.

Thanks to the success of Blink-182, Green Day, and The Offspring, punk is still hugely popular today.

23

CHAPTER THREE

RISE OF THE MACHINES

Ever since the rise of the electric guitar in the 1950s, developments in technology have influenced the way people make and play music. In the late 1970s and early 1980s, new types of electronic instruments changed music forever.

Electronic Movement

The first electronic synthesizers (keyboard-like instruments capable of creating **futuristic** sounds) appeared in the late 1960s. However, it wasn't until the end of the 1970s that they began to be widely used by musicians. At first, they were very expensive and hard to use. It was only when they became cheaper and more user-friendly that their popularity increased.

Kraftwerk

The pioneers of electronic music were a German pop band called Kraftwerk. During the 1970s, they released a series of albums made entirely of electronic sounds. Unlike most pop bands, Kraftwerk used synthesizers and early electronic drum machines rather than traditional instruments, such as guitars.

The Scoop

Kraftwerk had a huge effect on American hip-hop DJ and musician Afrika Bambaataa. He based his hip-hop hit "Planet Rock" on sections of the Kraftwerk tracks "Numbers" and "Trans Europe Express."

German producer Giorgio Moroder reinvented disco with Donna Summer's *I Feel Love*— a record made using only synthesizers.

In the 1980s, synth-pop bands, such as the Pet Shop Boys, became huge stars around the world.

New Bands, New Sounds

The futuristic sounds of Kraftwerk inspired many new musicians, particularly those in Sheffield, UK. There, bands such as The Human League and Cabaret Voltaire began making bleak electronic music using synthesizers they'd built themselves. These bands later had hits on the charts with a brand-new style called "synth-pop."

Drum Breakthroughs

In 1980, an electronics company called Roland released a drum machine named the TR-808. It proved to be one of the big musical breakthroughs of the 1980s. More affordable than previous drum machines, it was used by hip-hop producers to create a new sound called Electro. It was also used by dance music producers, disco musicians, and synth-pop bands.

Computers and Music

Synthesizers became more powerful in the early 1980s. During this period, many big recording studios offered musicians the chance to use early music computers, such as the Fairlight CMI and Synclavier. These cutting-edge instruments were very expensive and beyond the reach of most musicians. Those who could afford to used them to make some of the biggest-selling pop records of the time. Prince, R.E.M., U2, Madonna, Fleetwood Mac, and Hall and Oates were all users of the Fairlight CMI.

The influential Fairlight CMI bridged the gap between analog synthesizers and digital computers.

Massive Changes

Today, a whole new generation of synth-pop and indie-dance bands such as The Killers, Florence + the Machine, and Justice are gaining inspiration from 1980s synthesizer sounds. Huge pop records by artists such as Lady Gaga also use electronic keyboard sounds.

INDUSTRY CASE STUDY

MARRS

In 1987, a brand new electronic instrument called the digital sampler was first heard in popular music. A British band called MARRS used it to create a groundbreaking pop hit called "Pump Up the Volume." In doing so, they helped to change the way music was made forever.

Small Sample

The first **digital samplers** appeared in the early 1980s. To begin with, few people saw the potential of these machines. They allowed musicians to record, or "sample," small sections of other people's records, change them, and reuse them in their own records.

Cutting up Songs

The digital sampler was revolutionary because it meant that new music could be created using bits of previously recorded songs. Japanese electronics manufacturer Akai created its first digital samplers in the mid 1980s. By 1987 the process of "sampling" other people's records blew the industry apart.

Justified Art

One of the first bands to buy into the potential of the digital sampler was The Justified Ancients of Mu Mu, who later became the successful dance-pop band The KLF. The band created an album based entirely on samples of other people's records entitled *1987*.

Digital samplers such as this 1980s model by E-mu Systems allowed people with no musical training to make their own tracks.

Going to Court

The Justified Ancients of Mu Mu's *1987* was hailed by music critics as a dramatic step forward. The people whose records had been sampled disagreed. Pop group ABBA sued them, forcing the band to withdraw the record from stores. It was the first of many legal battles over music samples.

Sample Magic

The MARRS song, "Pump Up the Volume," became one of the most influential tracks in the United Kingdom and United States in the 1980s. It was the first successful hit single to be made almost entirely out of samples of other people's music. It used approximately 30 different samples from hip-hop, disco, Indian, funk, and dance records.

Copyright Issues

The impact of "Pump Up the Volume" was almost instant. It dominated clubs and rocketed to the higher reaches of the American and British charts. A number of artists whose music had been sampled, including producers Stock Aitken Waterman and James Brown, sued the band's record label 4AD for copyright infringement. MARRS was forced to hand over a portion of the money they earned from the record's success to the people whose music they'd sampled.

The Flood

The success of "Pump Up the Volume" paved the way for the use of sampling in popular music. In the months and years that followed, many pop, dance, and hip-hop producers used digital samplers

Public Enemy

MARRS wasn't the only band to see the potential of using a digital sampler to make new records. Hip-hop band Public Enemy made almost all of their music out of samples, adding their own raps over the top. Their hits "Rebel Without a Pause" and "Don't Believe the Hype" used sampled sounds, beats, and riffs.

to help them make new tracks. This type of sampling allowed people with no musical training to make music. It was the first step toward today's musical culture.

British pop stars The KLF were one of the first bands to see the potential of the digital sampler.

27

MUSIC MESSAGES

Music with a message didn't end with the decline of punk in 1979. Throughout the 1980s, rock and pop bands used music as a tool to talk about issues affecting their lives. They even used it to raise money for charity.

Bob Geldof was so shocked by the plight of starving African children, he put on a charity concert that raised $30 million.

Times are Tough

The 1980s were a tough time in the United States. Youth unemployment was high and the gap between the rich and poor was growing. Tensions between the United States and the Soviet Union (now Russia) meant that nuclear war was a very real threat.

Political Points

Just as in the 1960s and the late 1970s, many musicians responded to the difficulties in the world around them through music. From the "spooky" pop of The Specials' "Ghost Town," which was inspired by street riots, to Simply Red's "Money's Too Tight to Mention," many successful songs had a political message.

Charity Records

In 1984, people across the world were horrified by images of starving Africans that began appearing on television news reports. Many people wanted to help, and groups started raising money for charities working in Africa.

Two musicians decided they'd try to make a difference, as well. Bob Geldof and Midge Ure wanted to get together famous singers to make a record that could raise money for famine relief in Africa. That record was credited to Band Aid. It was called "Do They Know It's Christmas?"

Fight for Your Rights

The late 1980s saw a rise in hip-hop records that sought to educate American teenagers about the plight of black people in poor areas of cities. Public Enemy frontman Chuck D saw his music as a way of educating people about both black history and issues affecting the lives of millions of black Americans.

Changing the World

"Do They Know It's Christmas?" featured many of the biggest stars of the time, including members of bands such as Wham!, U2, Dire Straits, Duran Duran, and The Police. Even The Beatles member Paul McCartney made an appearance. The record sold over 1 million copies in the US alone. In 2004, a new version was made featuring Bono, Chris Martin, and Joss Stone.

American Idols

Following the success of "Do They Know It's Christmas?," a group of American stars got together in 1985 and made their own charity record to help starving Africans. The song they chose was called "We Are the World." It was written by Michael Jackson and Lionel Richie, and sung by an all-star cast including Stevie Wonder, Billy Joel, Bob Dylan, and Kenny Rogers.

Concert Success

On July 13, 1985, many of the biggest pop stars in the world performed at the Live Aid concerts at Wembley Stadium in London and at JFK Stadium in Philadelphia. The following day, the organizers announced that the concerts had raised more than $75 million for charity. In 2005, two more huge concerts took place in London and Philadelphia under the name Live 8, again featuring some of its decade's biggest stars.

The Scoop

Nelson Mandela had been in prison since 1962 for leading anti-apartheid movements in South Africa. In 1988, a tribute concert was organized to raise awareness of the problems in his country.

At the Nelson Mandela 70th Birthday Tribute, numerous artists performed to honor Mandela, as well as to raise awareness of his imprisonment.

29

HOUSE HITS

Rock and pop weren't the only styles of music undergoing huge changes in the 1980s. Dance music also had a revolution—one that continues to influence dance stars of today such as David Guetta, Fedde Le Grand, and Tiesto.

Dance music pioneer Kevin Saunderson is still a part of the techno scene to this day.

Future Sounds

In the summer of 1981 in Detroit, Michigan, a trio of high school friends began making their own electronic music at home. Using cheap synthesizers and drum machines, the trio of Juan Atkins, Derrick May, and Kevin Saunderson developed a futuristic electronic sound. Locals dubbed them "The Belleville Three," and by 1985, they had created a brand-new dance music—techno.

Warehouse Music

Meanwhile, in Chicago, Illinois, a trio of DJs was gaining a local reputation for using drum machines in their disco, hip-hop, and electro sets. At the Warehouse, Music Box, and Power Plant nightclubs, Ron Hardy, Lil' Louis, and Frankie Knuckles were laying the foundation for Chicago's own form of dance music, house.

House Trax

It wasn't long before these exciting new forms of electronic dance music from Chicago and Detroit started to get noticed across the

Between the late 1990s and early 2000s, superclubs such as Ministry of Sound made dance music big business.

Under a Groove

By the end of the decade, many variations of dance music had developed. Even rock bands were being influenced by dance music, with the British groups Happy Mondays and The Stone Roses at the center of a world famous **dance-rock fusion** scene.

The Scoop

The first house record to hit number one on the British pop charts was "Jack Your Body" by Chicago producer Steve "Silk" Hurley. It reached the top spot in January 1987, and kick-started the United Kingdom's love of house music.

The First House Record

In 1984, a teenager named Jesse Saunders made a 10-minute electronic dance track in his bedroom called "On and On." It was played regularly by Chicago's most important DJs. It is now widely thought of as the first-ever house record.

Dance Domination

New forms of dance music inspired by house and techno went on to dominate the pop charts for the early part of the 1990s and beyond. Much of today's dance music is still based on house and techno.

United States. Upon hearing these releases from pioneering record labels such as Trax, DJ International, Metroplex, and Transmat, record buyers across the country began to pick up on house and techno.

Rave On

The rise in house music made leading American and British nightclubs world famous. Eventually huge outdoor "raves" became popular with young people in the UK, many of whom took an illegal drug called Ecstasy. Later, raves spread across the Atlantic to the United States. The British government was worried about the effects of these raves and the drugs involved, so it soon drew up laws to ban them.

Rock bands such as the Happy Mondays were inspired by club culture, and their music had strong dance rhythms. They even employed a dancing "mascot" called Bez.

CHAPTER FOUR

POP WILL EAT ITSELF

Since the success of "Rapper's Delight" in 1979, hip-hop music has been on the fast-track to worldwide domination. Today, rap and R&B music rule the radio airwaves and pop charts. How did this happen?

East to West

Hip-hop pioneers such as Grandmaster Flash and the Furious Five, Kurtis Blow, Afrika Bambaataa, and KRS-One created an initial interest in rap music. This interest spread across the United States, and later the world, in the early 1980s.

Public Enemy's angry records showed rap tackle difficult subjects, such as poverty and racism.

New styles of rap music developed, with groups such as Public Enemy, Gang Starr, and N.W.A. using the music as a way of expressing their anger about the world around them, particularly life in poor inner-city areas.

Boys in the Hood

In 1986, a former punk-rock group called The Beastie Boys scored a hit with their rock-rap single "Fight for Your Right (to Party)." The record that followed, *Licensed to Ill*, became the first number-one rap album in the United States. Thanks to the efforts of The Beastie Boys and acts such as Run D.M.C., teenagers from white, black, and **Latino** communities could identify with hip-hop music. Rap record sales soared.

Former punk rockers The Beastie Boys took rap music to the masses in the late 1980s.

The Scoop

In the 1980s, clothes manufacturers spotted the potential to gain popularity by sponsoring rap acts. In 1986, Run D.M.C. signed a $1.8 million deal to advertise the Adidas brand. It was the first of many big money deals between rappers and clothing brands.

Worldwide Success

Since the 1990s, hip-hop has become one of the most popular styles of music around the world. There are rap scenes in many countries and even continents, with each region giving rap its distinct sound and style. Hip-hop beats and **production styles** have influenced other types of music, from indie-rock to house and dance.

Going Underground

Not everyone in the hip-hop community has enjoyed the music's mainstream success in recent years. Some rap artists and fans do not regard many of the world's biggest rap hits as true hip-hop records. As a result, a strong "underground hip-hop" scene has developed for those who want to stay true to the music's roots.

The popularity of breakdancing has increased as hip-hop has become a global musical force.

Culture Club

In the 1980s and 1990s, hip-hop appealed to teenagers. Not only was the music exciting and fresh, but there was also a whole culture they could buy into. Hip-hop was just as much about the clothes you wore and the quality of your breakdancing moves as it was about the music.

Superstars

In the last 20 years, many rappers have become global stars. With exposure from music videos, television appearances, and interviews, artists such as Eminem, Jay-Z, Sean "Diddy" Combs, Lil Wayne, Kanye West, and The Black Eyed Peas have sold huge amounts of records and become multimillionaires.

SUPERSTAR DJS

In the late 1990s and early 2000s, the dance music revolution started by Chicago and Detroit's producers became a huge global industry. For a brief period, a handful of DJs became the new rock stars.

Club Weekends

From the late 1980s, dance music grew in popularity around the world. The number of people going to nightclubs increased, and nightclubs became the focus of many people's weekends. As a result, DJs responded to the demand by making their own music. They became known as musical artists in their own right—entertainers who could create an atmosphere through the blend of music they played.

Club to the Studio

Many DJs with very little musical training used a combination of home computers and new music-making software to create their own dancefloor hits. DJ producers such as Fatboy Slim, The Chemical Brothers, and Daft Punk became stars with their own following. People bought their records, attended their club performances, and snatched up tickets for their **headline** appearances at dance music festivals.

Fatboy Slim is a pioneer of the big beat genre of dance music, typically driven by heavy breakbeats.

Superclubs!

In the 1990s, a number of "superclubs" were built to cater to the public's increased interest in dance music. Venues such as Twilo in New York City, Cream in Liverpool, UK, and Zouk in Singapore booked the biggest DJs in the world and became "must visit" destinations.

Big Money

A small group of DJs became very rich indeed. The likes of Carl Cox, Paul van Dyk, and Tiësto could earn big bucks for a two-hour DJ **set**. Some earned more in a weekend than many people could earn in an entire year. Sasha was once reportedly offered over $75,000 to play a New Year's Eve gig, but turned it down.

Back to the Underground

By 2005, a backlash had started against "superstar DJ" culture. A new generation of teenagers was more inspired by underground, alternative rock music and hip-hop. The dance music industry suffered and returned to its underground roots. Since then, new headline DJs have appeared, but they are nowhere in reach of re-creating the "superstar DJs" craze of the 1990s and 2000s.

Lasting Legacy

The rise of the DJ and dance music culture over the past 30 years has left lasting marks on modern music. Without pioneers such as Sasha, Fatboy Slim, and Paul Oakenfold,

today's top DJ producers would not be able to live such a celebrity way of life. Now, headline DJs such as David Guetta, Armin van Buuren, and Tiësto are treated like rock stars. There may be fewer superstars than there were 10 years ago, but DJs are as important to music as ever.

The Scoop

In July 2002, Fatboy Slim played a free DJ set on the beach of his hometown in Brighton, UK. Organizers expected around 60,000 people to turn up. In the end, an estimated 250,000 people crowded onto the beach to hear his performance—a first in the history of DJing.

As the world's most popular "superstar DJ," Tiësto was asked to play at the opening ceremony of the 2004 Olympics.

35

ROCK REVIVAL

Since the early 1990s, rock music has risen again in popularity. This is due to the mainstream success of alternative and indie artists, many of whom were inspired by rock's past.

Rock Dinosaurs

At the tail end of the 1980s, rock was viewed as old-fashioned. Crossover dance records and "manufactured" pop artists such as New Kids on the Block and Kylie Minogue dominated the airwaves.

Nirvana's grunge rock sound and appearance transformed rock music and fashion in the 1990s.

Youth Movement

New sound came in the form of grunge, a style of alternative rock that grew up around Seattle, Washington. Featuring **distorted guitar sounds**, raw music, and lyrics that dealt with the depressing side of life, the music of bands such as Soundgarden, Pearl Jam, Alice in Chains, and Sonic Youth hit a nerve with young people around the world.

Shift to Mainstream

The album that marked grunge's movement into mainstream music was *Nevermind* by Seattle band Nirvana. Hailed as a rock masterpiece by critics, it replaced Michael Jackson's *Dangerous* at the top of the American album charts in 1992.

Reinventing Rock

Many grunge bands were inspired by 1960s **garage rock** and 1980s hardcore punk. Meanwhile, in the United Kingdom, a new wave of bands arrived with a different influence: the classic British music of the 1960s.

Cool Britannia

Influenced by bands like The Beatles, The Kinks, and The Rolling Stones, 1990s "Britpop" bands such as Blur, Oasis, and Pulp had huge success with their reinventions of classic 1960s rock. American music magazines hailed the influence of these bands as a "second British invasion," mirroring the impact of The Beatles in the 1960s.

After Punk

In recent years, many bands on both sides of the Atlantic have successfully reinvented a lesser-known type of music from New York called post-punk. The early 1980s original fused punk with sounds of the city's dance music scene. Today, bands such as LCD Soundsystem, The Rapture, and The Futureheads successfully combine the same musical elements.

The Scoop

In the summer of 1995, Blur and Oasis began a conflict known as the "Battle of Britpop." The rivals released new singles on the same day in a heated competition. In the end, Blur won as its song "Country House" hit the number-one spot with Oasis' "Roll With It" coming in second place.

British bands Blur (above) and Oasis (below) fought a bitter battle for chart supremacy in 1995.

New and Old

Since the end of Britpop in the early 2000s, many other forms of alternative rock music have flourished. American "nu punk" bands such as Blink-182 and Green Day have enjoyed global success, while Rage Against the Machine and The Red Hot Chili Peppers have also had success by including influences from funk and classic hip-hop.

37

MAKING ARTISTS

Ever since the early days of modern music, popular music has had its fair share of **manufactured** stars and **hit factories**. In recent years, big record labels have used television shows to encourage viewers to join in the hit-making process and choose their own pop stars.

Hit Factories

The term "manufactured pop" is often used to describe bands or artists whose careers are controlled by big record labels. While these artists may be talented singers, they are usually unknown artists molded to fit a certain purpose or role. **Management companies** or **record company executives** take them on for their look and potential appeal to music buyers.

The Money Men

Two men who have great experience creating successful manufactured pop bands are Simon Fuller and Simon Cowell. These British businessmen were behind some of the biggest pop acts of the 1990s and 2000s, including The Spice Girls and Il Divo.

The X Factor has been a huge television ratings smash on both sides of the Atlantic.

Popstars

Fuller and Cowell used a television show called *Popstars* to put together a new manufactured pop band. Viewers voted for their favorite contestants until a band was created. The winners—Hear'Say—were given the prize of a recording contract.

Ratings Success

Fuller and Cowell's idea was a huge ratings success. A number of other shows followed the same successful idea, including *American Idol*, *America's Got Talent*, *The Voice*, and *The X Factor*. In many cases, the winner's debut single has hit the top spot on the American or British charts.

Not a Fan...

Not all music fans enjoy these reality television shows and their effect on popular music. In 2009, a campaign was organized on the Internet to prevent that year's *X Factor* single from securing the prized Christmas number-one slot on the British pop charts.

Global Icons

Although only a very small number of today's music stars started their careers by appearing on reality television shows, these shows have helped to create a number of genuine pop stars, including British singers Leona Lewis and Susan Boyle, and American artists Kelly Clarkson and Carrie Underwood.

Buying in the Name

The campaign was hugely popular with fans of alternative and underground music. They hated the sort of manufactured pop produced by Cowell's *X Factor* and *Got Talent* shows. Many bands and musicians supported the campaign, and Rage Against the Machine's rock anthem, "Killing in the Name," sold enough copies to send it to the top of the charts. The band donated all the profits from sales to charity.

The Scoop

Susan Boyle became a worldwide sensation after appearing on Britain's Got Talent in 2009. Within a week of her first performance on the show, clips of her appearance had been viewed over 100 million times on YouTube. Her first album went on to top the US Billboard chart for six straight weeks, and it sold 3 million copies in 2009.

Kelly Clarkson was one of the first reality TV contestants to become a global pop sensation.

The iPod

In the last decade, the way people buy and listen to music has changed greatly. Now we can find, buy, and listen to music on mobile phones, tablets, and many other portable devices. This change was kick-started by a revolutionary product—the iPod.

The success of the iPod has changed the way we buy, listen to, and share music.

MP3 Magic

In 1998, software developers in the United States announced that they'd come up with a new way of storing music on computers—MP3 files. These were small and took up very little space on a computer's hard drive, meaning that PC and Mac users could easily build huge libraries of songs. A number of electronics companies launched portable MP3 players that were capable of storing a small selection of songs. They proved popular with hardcore computer users, but did not sell in big numbers.

Faster Internet

Computer users began to see the potential of MP3 files when faster Internet connections arrived around 2000. Now, they could easily download MP3 files from music-sharing websites.

Digital Pirates

The music industry reacted strongly to what it called "Internet piracy." They were particularly annoyed by Napster, a service that allowed people to swap digital music files for free. Suddenly, any track became free of charge.

Steve Jobs' Vision

Apple Computer co-founder Steve Jobs saw the potential of MP3s and the Internet as a way of distributing and selling music. He wanted to create a portable music player that could store large amounts of music. He thought there would be a market for a device that could hold at least 1,000 songs.

iPod Is a Hit

Steve Jobs was right. Apple launched the iPod digital music player in September 2001, and it was an immediate success. Despite being quite expensive, sales were quick.

Goodbye CDs

By 2003, Jobs was ready to launch the next phase of his plan: the iTunes Store. This innovation allowed iPod users to buy music files legally and download them directly to their iPod devices. Users would be able to buy individual songs if they wished, as well as whole albums. For the first time, music fans could pick and choose what they wanted to buy and listen to —they no longer had to buy an entire CD to get the one track they wanted.

iPod Mania

The same time that the iTunes store launched, Apple announced a new range of iPods that could be used with PC computers. Sales of iPods soared, and soon more people were buying music downloads than CDs. To date, nearly 400 million iPods have been sold worldwide.

The late Steve Jobs' "big idea" has made Apple one of the richest companies in the world.

TIMELINE: The iPod

1998: The first widely available portable MP3 player, the MPMan, is launched

2001: Apple launches the first iPod with a capacity of 1,000 songs

2003: iTunes Music Store launches

2007: Apple launches the iPhone, a mobile telephone and iPod combined

2010: Apple announces it has sold over 275 million iPods since 2001

2011: iTunes Store sells its 16 billionth song

41

POWER TO THE PEOPLE

Since rock and roll shook the music industry to its foundations in the 1950s, popular music has changed beyond recognition. Thanks to the Internet and other advances in technology, music fans and amateur producers are shaping the future of music.

Closed Shop

Less than 30 years ago, music was controlled by a small group of major record labels, a handful of music magazines, and a string of popular radio stations. Labels carefully chose the releases, journalists wrote about them, and radio stations played the music. Mainstream music fans had little choice regarding what they listened to.

Computer Music

Things began to change in the 1990s when computers became more powerful and affordable. Suddenly, software became available that allowed enthusiastic young musicians to make their own music. They didn't need to spend money on hiring out record studios—they could do it all in their bedrooms.

Download This!

The Internet changed everything. Artists could now easily **distribute** music around the world as MP3 files. There was no need to buy CDs or vinyl records when you could spend a few cents on a brand-new song, or even download one for free.

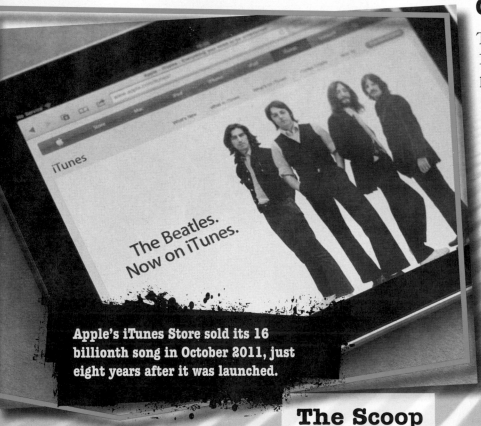

Apple's iTunes Store sold its 16 billionth song in October 2011, just eight years after it was launched.

The Scoop

Several teenage musicians have received big record contracts after posting their tracks on the video-sharing website YouTube. Superstar Justin Bieber was discovered by manager Scooter Braun in 2008 when Braun saw his video online.

Social Upheaval

The Internet has made it easier for young musicians to get their songs heard by many more people, and for new trends to develop more quickly. Now, you could make a track in an evening, upload it to the Internet, and get feedback in minutes.

No More Record Labels

The Internet has also allowed musicians to bypass record labels. Now, bands can sell their songs through websites such as Bandcamp. Some big artists, such as Radiohead, have even experimented with giving away their music to fans for free.

Online services such as Spotify and YouTube make it easy to listen to whatever you want, whenever you want.

World Music

All these changes in technology and communication mean that previously tiny local trends and musical styles can spread around the world in weeks, days, or hours. For example, in 2011 British clubs went crazy for the sounds of Juke and Footstep, two obscure forms of dance music made in Chicago, Illinois. Instrumental hip-hop changed dramatically in 2010 and 2011, too, thanks to the experimental production techniques of artists variously based in Los Angeles, Scotland, and Portugal.

Global Groove

It is now possible for bedroom musicians to build up a huge following around the world without spending a single penny. What's more, music fans now have more choice than ever before. New forms of music can take hold on the Internet in days or weeks and change again within a few months. All this has made the world of modern music more exciting than ever. We've never had it so good!

The Internet music revolution has allowed bands such as Radiohead to sell or give away their music directly to fans.

GLOSSARY

acoustic non-electric instruments, for example, a traditional acoustic guitar

alternative rockers people who make or listen to alternative or underground rock music

assassination term used to describe the murder of a high profile figure such as a president, politician, or head of state

backing track the music over which an MC "raps" or a singer sings

bass line a sequence of low, deep musical notes often used as part of a song's backing track. The bass line helps to give the song rhythm and momentum.

block parties outdoor, music and dance events held in local parks and other open spaces

chords groups of musical notes played at the same time

credited to to say someone is responsible for making something, for example, a record

dance-rock fusion music that uses elements of both traditional rock and electronic dance music

digital sampler an electronic machine used to record—"sample"—and edit sounds or short excerpts from recordings

distorted guitar sounds strange and fuzzy sounds made using an electric guitar and a special effects unit

distribute to get a product—for example, a record—to stores to sell

editing the process of cutting and rearranging pre-recorded music or film using tape or, computer software

experimental trying to do things in new, different, or unconventional ways

folk a traditional form of music that developed over hundreds of years

funk a heavy form of dance music that originated in African-American communities in the late 1960s and early 1970s

fuse join together

futuristic something that looks or sounds innovative or from the future

garage rock a loose and noisy form of rock music that has its origins in the bedrooms and garages of 1960s America

gospel songs religious music traditionally sung in church

headliner refers to a band or DJ that is the main attraction at a concert or festival

hit factories recording studios that specialize in making hit pop records

horn musical slang for brass instruments, such as trumpet, trombone, and saxophone

iconic a moment or person that goes down in history

jazz an inventive style of music created by black musicians using traditional instruments, such as saxophone, trumpet, drums, and piano

Latin music influenced by the sounds of South America, such as samba and mambo

Latino term used to refer to Americans whose families originally came from Central and South American countries

looping techniques the process of repeating a pre-recorded sound or musical section using a tape machine or computer program

LSD an illegal drug that causes people to view the world in a strange way, and can cause serious brain damage

mainstream popular with a lot of people

management companies firms who specialize in managing the affairs of music, television, or film stars, for example, negotiating contracts and coming up with strategies to make them more successful

manufactured pop music designed to appeal to a particular group of people, or to as many different people as possible

mind-altering drugs or substances that change the way people view the world

pioneers people who do something first

production styles methods of making, recording, and producing music

psychedelic term used to refer to the effects of certain illegal drugs, such as LSD, and music made by people who experiment with those drugs

"quick mix" mixing the process of quickly alternating between music stored on vinyl records played on two different turntables

race laws laws in the United States that restricted black people from the same rights as white people

racist system racism built into the way a country is run

record company executives people who manage big record labels—companies who specialize in selling music

record producer a person who specializes in recording and producing music

revolutionary an action that is so different and monumental that it changes the way people think, do something, or live their lives

rhythm and blues a popular form of music made using guitars and drums that was originally invented by black musicians

set the list of songs that a band or DJ performs in concert

trademark sound the musical style of a band, singer, or record label that listeners can identify them by (for example, the Motown soul sound)

underground less well–known

Vietnam War a long-running and unpopular war in Vietnam, Asia (1955–1975). American armed forces joined the conflict in 1965.

FURTHER READING

Books

Bill Brewster & Frank Broughton. *The Record Players: DJ Revolutionaries* (Black Cat, 2010).

Melanie J. Cornish. *The History of Hip-Hop* (Crabtree, 2009).

Nelson George. *Where Did Our Love Go?: The Rise and Fall of the Motown Sound* (University of Illinois, 2007).

Mark Mussari. *American Life and Music: From Elvis Presley to Lady Gaga* (Marshall Cavendish Benchmark, 2013).

Simon Reynolds. Retromania: *Pop Culture's Addiction to Its Own Past* (Faber & Faber, 2011).

Websites

Read about the history of technology in the music industry from the PBS show Frontline. **www.pbs.org/wgbh/pages/frontline/ shows/music/inside/cron.html**

Read stories about the history of popular culture. **www.pophistorydig.com**

Note to parents and teachers
Every effort has been made by the publisher to ensure that these websites contain no inappropriate or offensive material. However, because of the nature of the Internet, it is impossible to guarantee that the contents of these sites will not be altered. We strongly advise that Internet access is supervised by a responsible adult.

INDEX